INSTANT EULOGY

A time to weep,
and a time to laugh;
a time to mourn,
and a time to dance.

-- Ecclesiastes 3:4

INSTANT EULOGY

Complete instructions on how to write a eulogy,
plus tips on how to plan a funeral

By Mike Mercuré

Instant Eulogy
Complete instructions on how to write a eulogy, plus tips on how to plan a funeral
By Mike Mercuré

Printed in the United States of America

Contents

Introduction

By Mike Mercuré
copyright © 2010 Anchor Publishing

If you have been asked to write a eulogy, this probably means you were an important part of this person's life. You have a enormous responsibility to honor this person. Writing the eulogy will probably be one of the most important things you will ever have to do.

The help and advice in this book will guide you in writing an exceptional eulogy. First, you should realize that this is an emotionally challenging task to perform. If you become overwhelmed by emotion, stop and take a few minutes to yourself. You have just incurred a great loss and cannot be expected to maintain your composure at all times.

Traditionally, eulogies have been used to honor and pay tribute to the person who has died. As long as you accomplish this in your speech, feel free to format the speech as you wish. Don't be intimidated by this daunting task! If you follow the key steps outlined in this guide you will be able to write a eulogy you can be proud of.

This is probably a busy time as you are preparing to lay this person to rest and you might be thinking about how to actually get started writing the eulogy. Try taking fifteen minutes each day just to gather your thoughts and hopes about the speech. This way, you'll find inspiration in your thoughts and the writing process may begin.

*Our fear of death is like our fear
that summer will be short,
but when we have had our swing of
pleasure, our fill of fruit,
and our swelter of heat,
we say we have had our day.*

-- Ralph Waldo Emerson

Part 1

Eulogies

There is no goal better than this one: to know as you lie on your deathbed that you lived your true life, and you did whatever made you happy.

– Steve Chandler

Chapter 1

Eulogy Speeches

Steps to Take:

1. Decide what you want to convey in the eulogy.

2. Figure out how you want to actually convey it.

3. Take the time to sit down and write the speech!

4. Practice again and again!

5. Deliver the speech.

Eulogy Speeches – Steps to Take

Eulogy Step 1

When you first begin to write your speech, think about what you want to accomplish in your eulogy. Do you want to talk about all the professional accomplishments of the person you are eulogizing? Do you want it to read like an informal biography? Or do you just want to share a few memories you have had with that person? Once you decide what your goal is, draft a speech that will fulfill your goal. Remember that it is of utmost importance to honor the person who has passed on. The first step in writing your eulogy is to collect your thoughts. Think of specific items you definitely want to include in the eulogy.

Eulogy Step 2

Second, once the ceremony is arranged, you can determine what kind of tone you would like to set. Think about what kind of tone you want for the eulogy. There are several to choose from including serious, solemn, sentimental or even humorous. Choose a tone that most suits the character of the person you are eulogizing and take into consideration the events surrounding the death. Some people may think that they can only speak well of the person and events transpired in the person's life. However, don't be afraid of mentioning things that were not the highlights. After all, it is a combination of positive and negative things that makes a life complete. As long as you are still honoring and paying tribute to the person, it is appropriate to mention these things. Pay attention to important things like word choice and structure because these are key items in a successful speech.

Eulogy Step 3

Though it may seem too painful or difficult, you must actually make the time to sit down and begin to compose your speech. The most difficult parts to write may be the beginning and the end. If you find you are at a loss for words, you may want to try a method called stream of consciousness. This is where you simply write down anything going through your mind. Most likely you will have written down some material you can use. Though it will definitely need serious editing and organization, the important thing is that you have it on paper. Try just getting down all of your thoughts on paper and then sort them into categories or subjects.

If you choose to emphasize the accomplishments of the person, write it so they flow smoothly and in sequence. You may want to select a theme for the eulogy. A theme could be something that person loved doing or something that they were known for. For example, if the person liked to knit you could relate various stories or qualities they had back to knitting.

A common way to begin a eulogy is with a proverb, a quotation or a poem. If you find one that reminds you of a person, then use it. In the bonus section of this book you will find many serious and humorous quotations dealing with the subjects of death, grieving and life.

Though it may take some time to read through all of them, you will most likely find them useful. If you find one that strikes you, then find a way to work into your eulogy or read it at the ceremony. Look for quotes that remind you of your loved one. These quotes are a short, eloquent and touching way to summarize your thoughts or feelings.

Another effective technique in a eulogy is the use of a personal story or anecdote. These personal experiences are excellent ways to honor the deceased.

Here are a few techniques you can use in a eulogy:

✓ A list of accomplishments
✓ A condensed biography
✓ A collection of anecdotes or experiences you had with that person
✓ How you are feeling
✓ Promises and pledges

Eulogy Step 4

Now that you have written your speech, practice it. The more you practice the speech, the easier it will be to read. Thoroughly practicing the speech is essential to making it successful! Practice your speech as much as possible. Any time you have a few free minutes go through it. Try practicing in front of other people so that you get an idea of what it is going to be like. Even if you think you know it, keep on practicing. Words often run smoothly in your head but do not come out as well out loud especially in an emotion packed atmosphere.

Maintain eye contact with your practice audience and avoid distracting body movements or fidgeting as you present your eulogy. Remember to take your time delivering the speech. Pause when you want to emphasize a point and want the audience to think it over or laugh.

Though it might be difficult, try to imagine the reaction of the person you are eulogizing. Do you think he/she would be happy? Satisfied? Disappointed? Adjust your speech accordingly. Think about whether the eulogy conveys the message you want.

Eulogy Step 5

Actually delivering the speech may be the most terrifying for some people. Do whatever it takes to be comfortable in front of everyone. If you need water or tissues with you, don't hesitate to bring them. It is natural to be overcome with emotion so it is acceptable to cry or just take a moment to compose yourself. Just remember that everyone at the funeral empathizes with you and will support you through this difficult time. Try and remain calm, speak clearly and loudly. Make sure to stay hydrated and avoid caffeine before giving your speech.

Remember:
People want to hear:

- What kind of a person was he/she?
- What drove this person?
- What did they accomplish in their lives?
- What are they leaving behind?
- What will be missed?

They DO NOT need to hear:
How many mistakes he/she made.
Any irrelevant information.

In this book you will find sample eulogies for family members and friends. They are just examples of how you may want to model your speech. **The best advice for your speech is to make it as personal as possible!** Use any experiences or memories that stand out in your mind that made this person unique.

Remember to **take a deep breath** and **stay focused** on the task at hand before giving your speech! Keep in mind that you are doing this to honor and remember the person who has passed away...so give it all you've got!

Chapter 2

Sample Eulogies

How to use these samples

Don't confine yourself to reading only the samples for each of the people below.
If your mother died, there may be very nice and applicable sample statements in the father section or the sister section. We have written this book so you don't have to think too much in this emotionally strained time. Combine statements from any of the examples to create a eulogy perfect for your loved one.

We have put tips in the sample eulogies to

remind you to substitute information specific to your loved one.
Your best bet is to review all the different sample eulogies in this book and select sections that you like. Arrange them in order on a separate piece of paper and you will have an instant outline of your eulogy. Then go back and select the stories, statements, pledges and information that fit your loved one.

Select a quote the fits your situation.
You will also want to spend time reviewing the quotation section to select a quote the fits your situation perfectly.

Sample Eulogies

There are two sample eulogies for each of the following people. Remember: You can select nice statements from any of the samples below and combine them to create your very special custom eulogy:

Tip: Visit the serious quote section below or the humorous quote section below and/or use one of your loved one's favorite poems. They can be inserted at the beginning, the middle or the end of your eulogy.

In the next pages, you will find eulogies for:

- Mother
- Father
- Son
- Daughter
- Sister
- Brother
- Friend
- Husband
- Wife
- Grandmother
- Grandfather

Mother

Insert your mother's story.
My mother was a wonderful woman. She lived her life with the courage and purpose most people strive for. She had an incredible spirit that persevered through anything.

My mother's life began in a small town in Maryland. She was the third child and was adored by her parents and older sisters. She was a gifted student and well liked by her classmates. While attending the University of Maryland, she met my father. They married two years later. My father was the love of her life. They started out as two young kids who were ambitious and hopeful that their love would carry them through anything.

Soon after, my older sister was born. My father and mother struggled to keep food on the table but there was always plenty of love and care in our home. My mother chose to spend her days at home devoting her life to her children and husband. Despite dreams she may have had for herself and her career, she turned her focus to our family. Mom always did that. She always sacrificed her own needs for those of our family or loved ones. We never really knew how much she had sacrificed for us until much later.

Insert what you learned from your mother.
Mom taught me many valuable lessons about life and people. Most importantly, she loved and supported us. I remember when I was cut from the baseball team and when I was not accepted to my dream college. She wiped away my tears and told me she loved me no matter what. She made me feel as if I could do no wrong. She was proud of me simply for being me.

She had this amazing capability to just love people and make them feel special. We will all miss her compassion, her spirit and her love. In her last few years, she endured much physical suffering. In a way I am glad that she is free from the pain. I know that she would have smiled if she could see us all gathered here for her. I promise her that we will always love her and keep her in our hearts and minds.

Mother

My mother is probably the best friend I ever had. She was with me in both the good and bad times of my life. No matter where she was or what she was doing, if she heard I was in trouble, she would come running to help and comfort me.

Insert a well known quality about your mother.

Her generosity at times brought tears to my eyes. She was a kind person who would give me her share of the food, even if there were none left for her.

She was wonderful and very easy to get along with. Everyone who knew her — friends, relatives, neighbors, co-workers — loved her and praised her for her loving and helpful ways.

Insert more about her life.

She was very kind and generous to me. My older brother and sister always complained that I was her favorite, but I know she loved us all equally. She was a housewife and a career woman who always took care of her husband and children throughout her life without complaining. She was a great cook and would often come up with new recipes. She was confident and knew how to handle things well.

Insert her history.

She was born and raised in a small town in Pittsburgh, where she completed her education at the University of Pennsylvania. After graduation, she married my father and they decided to start their own family. She supported my father through rough times when there was not enough food for the next meal and kept the atmosphere healthy with her love and support.

It is the result of her blessings and prayers that I became successful in my life and accomplished so much. I am thankful to her and I will miss her a lot. Sweet memories of her will always remain in our hearts and thoughts.

Father

Insert a memory of a special time you had with your father as a child.

Today, I will try to tell all of you how much my father meant to me and pay tribute to his life. I would like to do this by sharing one of my favorite memories of him.

When I was seven, we went on a car trip driving through Canada. We packed up our old, worn out station wagon with as much luggage as we could fit and went on our way. We stopped at local parks and camped out several nights in a row. My father, delighted to be in nature's purest form and surrounded by its beauty, would stand there in awe of the picturesque sceneries.

It was during these camping trips that I truly experienced my father's innovation and creativity. He could make the woods seem like a five star hotel without losing the feeling of nature.

Name your father's good qualities.

Many years later, my father told me he wanted us to experience nature and all its power so we could appreciate it. My father always valued beauty and beautiful things. This meant he had great respect for cycle of life and all living things. He was never afraid of death or dying, he just accepted it is as part of life. He was the bravest man I know.

State how you felt about your father as you became an adult.

Apart from being such a wonderful father, he was also a great friend. As I became older I often sought his advice and guidance on matters in my adult life. I was able to talk to my father about anything. As a child, you do not always realize that your parents are individuals and that at one point they each had their own hopes and dreams. I enjoyed getting to know my father as the man he was and not simply my father. And I am proud to say that he was my father.

My mother always said that Dad was hard to understand but easy to love and now after all these years I truly know what she means. We will miss you Dad and we hope your soul can take flight in the woods where you can be free.

Son

It has always been a mother's worst fear to bury her child. Today I am faced with this grim task.

Recall how you felt when your son was a baby.

I remember what it felt like when I first held Sam in my arms and the joy I felt. I loved him the minute I laid eyes on him. I knew we were about to begin an adventure.

Recall the type of child he was.

He was a fearless child who tried anything and often made mischief in the process. Everyone who knew him loved him.

Now, we are faced with the difficult question of how to move on with our lives. And, for this answer I look to Sam. I know he would have wanted us to continue our lives but to never forget him. And, I know that we will keep his spirit alive by keeping him in our hearts and thoughts.

Recall more of your son's personality traits.
Sam always said life was too short to care about

what other people think, and to do what your heart wants. I always admired Sam's courage. He had the courage to follow his heart, which very few people have. He lived his life with thought and purpose. Sam had a clear idea of what he wanted to accomplish in his life. Though his life was cut short, I believe he had already done most of what he set out to do.

Recall something your son taught you.

Sam can live on with us through the things that he taught us all. He taught me that self-forgiveness is as important as self-love. He taught me to never give up even when things seem hopeless. And, of course, he taught me to always try to discover new things. Besides giving me the unconditional love that only children can give, he always gave something me to be proud of. Sam, I am still proud of you and always will be.

Sam was my first child and one of my greatest accomplishments. We will all miss him greatly, but we know he is with us every step of the way. We hope he will find what he was looking for and that he may rest in peace.

Son

Recall the actual birth experience of your son.

My son was my pride and joy. He was a God-given gift that brought happiness and joy in our life. When my wife delivered him prematurely, both their lives were in danger. They said it was a question of saving either the mother or the child. Fortunately by God's grace, things went well and both of them were saved. It was a miracle for the doctors, too.

Recall a funny personality trait of your son.

Right from his childhood he was notorious for doing every possible thing he could to make a mess. He always did things far above the normal capabilities of any other child his age.

Recall a story that illustrates the above personality.

One day when he was eight, he opened our tape recorder and disassembled each and every nut and bolt to clean it. He then went on to reassemble it neatly without even telling anybody. Then when his mother asked if he had been doing his homework he said no and was scolded. I still remember the expression on his face as he came running to me wiping tears from his eyes. With his hand pointed towards his mother while he was explaining that she was mad at him. It would take hours for them to make up. And then things would be back to normal again and he would be up to some other mischief.

Recall one of your son's best traits.

Despite being so naughty, he was very sharp and intelligent. He always surprised everyone in his class including his teachers and friends. Of course, when his results came out, he would score the highest in the whole class. His teachers used to say that with his writing skills he should become a poet one day because he writes so well.

State your heartfelt feelings.

I just cannot fathom the loss of my son and am not sure what I am going to do. I will miss him for the rest of my life.

Daughter

Tell how you felt when your daughter was a baby.

I could never have asked for a better daughter. Samantha fulfilled all the dreams Jill and I had for our children. She always gave us something to be proud of and a reason to smile. She was the sweetest baby. She slept through the night and never cried too much. Everyone asked what we did to make her such an agreeable baby, and we just had to give her the credit because she did it all on her own.

Tell how you couldn't help but spoil her.

I knew from day one that she was going to be daddy's little girl. Jill always told me that I was going to spoil her and that I had to put my foot down. But every time she looked at me with those big brown eyes, my heart just melted and I couldn't say no to her.

Tell how she grew up to be wonderful.

Despite my giving in to her every whim, Samantha grew up to become a lovely young woman. She was an excellent student who was well liked by her peers. She was an assertive, independent woman who knew what she wanted and went after it. I admired her for following her dreams and staying determined and confident along the way.

Tell how you felt when she got married.

When Samantha told us that she was getting married, it was a bittersweet moment. She was no longer just our little girl but was going to be a wife and eventually a mother. We could not have been happier once we met Todd, and we felt reassured that she was in good hands. They lived happily together and had their own children, Mike and Sarah. But she could not stay with us to be their mother, Todd's wife and our daughter.

Express how her memory will live on.

Now we must figure out a way to go on without her here physically, but we know her spirit is always near. We will keep her with us through the memories and moments we all had with her.

Samantha wanted it all. She wanted the career and the family and though people told her this was impossible, she managed to do it. She didn't just do it, she did it well.

Talk directly to her.
Samantha, you will always be our little girl. We love you and we will miss you

Daughter

Express your extreme pain.

It is very painful that my daughter is no longer with us. I really have no idea how to deal with it because her smiles and actions haunt me. I can still hear her voice echoing in my ears.

Talk about her nickname.

My daughter Komal was the youngest in the family. She was loved by all and brought up with great care. She had several nicknames in our family. I used to call her "gudiya," which means doll in our native Hindi language. Her mother used to call her "Komu," which is short form for Komal. Sometimes her brother teased her by calling her "fatty." He was very skinny in comparison to her. This resulted in an argument and they would not talk to each other for a few hours.

Talk about her great accomplishments.

My daughter was so sweet. All her family and friends loved her. She was so brilliant that she finished college at the age of 20. She was honored with the award for best student of the year at her graduation ceremony. When her name was called in front of the 40,000 people in the stadium, it brought tears to my eyes. I could not have been more proud of her. It was then that I realized that our daughter had grown up and that she would be stepping out in the real world to face new challenges in life. Who knew what fate had in store for us all.

Talk about her career and family.

Just two years after graduation, she got her first job. She soon married Alan, the general manager of Ford Motors. Two years later she gave birth to a beautiful baby boy. Though everything seemed happy, a storm came into our life and took our daughter from us.

Talk about your disbelief and explanation of why this may have happened.

It is hard for me and everybody else to believe that Komal has left us so early. I am sure Alan and the baby are grieving in a way none of us can understand. It was their dream to become parents and raise their child the same way they had been brought up. Fate has led them to this destiny. We will miss her greatly.

Sister

Talk about your life with her when you were children.

My sister was my first friend, my first playmate and my idol. I looked up to her from day one. I would do everything she did, and tried to play with her and her friends. I know this annoyed her but she always let me tag along. Even as we grew up I still did everything to try and be more like her. I could not have asked for a better role model.

Talk about your sister's wonderful traits and skills.

Elizabeth was a dedicated and talented person who excelled at everything she did. Everyone turned to her for advice. She helped with everything from dating and friendships to cooking the perfect casserole. She was an extremely well rounded person, knowledgeable about the arts and culture and also about where to buy the cheapest vegetables.

Select one really great trait and expand upon it.

Her approachability and charm always drew people to her. She will be sorely missed for her wise words and spirit. Elizabeth loved life and treasured those around her. She was one of the most popular girls in school and in college. She always had many friends. She always remembered everyone's individual likes and dislikes. And, she remembered everyone's unique story.

Today is dedicated to remembering her story. It is a story of woman with a pure and beautiful heart who was loved for her kindness and warmth. She will be remembered as a great friend, a beloved wife and mother, a cherished

Recall a story of when you and your sister were children.

When I was gathering her belongings I found a picture album of our vacation we took when we were 8 and 10 years old. That summer we went camping in the local park. In the picture she had her arm wrapped around my shoulder and we were both grinning widely. Suddenly, memories of our time together came back to me. I know that even now she has her arm wrapped around me to hold me and love me as long I live.

Promise that her family will be taken care of.

Today, she leaves behind a family of her own. I promise her that David and the children John and Jane will be taken care of. John and Jane remind me so much of their mother. She will continue to live with us through them and our memories of her.

Sister

Share a memory of your sister and something you really appreciated about her.

My sister was a gift given to all of us by God. I have wonderful memories of her. We used to enjoy each other's company a lot and share our secrets with each other. We always had a good time. One thing I appreciated about her was that she always supported me as a sister and as friend. She allowed me to play with her friends and her whether they liked it or not. I always tried to follow her good qualities and advice.

Share her background and accomplishments.

She managed her home with love and care, all the while establishing a successful career as a journalist. She was very intelligent and always passed her exams with flying colors and she was first in her class. She was very active in sports and other extracurricular activities. She was the Student President of her college and she told me that was one of the biggest professional accomplishments of her life. She was a great daughter to our parents and a wonderful sister, a beloved wife and a dedicated mother.

44

Share a memory of a significant life event and tell how you felt.

I still remember the day she was married and how sad I felt at the thought of being separated from my sister. She was my best friend who I could always rely on. She tried to convince me that even though she was leaving the house, her memories would always remain there in the house.

Promise that her family will be taken care of.

And, now that the day has come when she has left this world, her words still echo in my mind. I miss her a lot. Her death is a great loss for everyone including her husband John and her children Amy and Mary, who often remind us of her. It is our duty to take care of those children with great love and affection. This will be our way of continuing to honor her throughout their lives.

Brother

Talk about how your brother looked out for you and how you are going look out for his family.

My older brother Jake was the kind of brother that everyone wanted. He was overprotective but only because he cared. Every time I went out I got the same lecture from him. Don't do anything you don't want to and if some boy bothers you, tell me and I will take care of him.

Jake always took care of everyone and protected those he cared about. It is our turn to look after those now that Jake is no longer able to. This means that his wife Maureen and children Justin, Bob, Margaret and Donna have all of our love and support.

Remember an argument you had as children and then turn it around as insignificant compared to the wonderful time you spent with your brother.

I am sure that his wife and children are aware of what a loving man their father was. But this gathering today should remind you that many other people loved him. He was a gentle and

46

caring man. I remember during one summer vacation at the beach we got into a particularly bad fight. We were fighting over who should get to bury who in the sand. Finally, he gave in when I threatened to go and cry to our parents. Five minutes later we were happily playing in the sand together.

Despite whatever disagreements or fights we had, we always made up because we were playmates. Then as we became older we became good friends. I turned to him as a friend and someone who could help guide me during these difficult years of life. No matter what time I called, he would always make time to talk with me and offer me advice.

You can always tease about a well known trait to let people laugh a little.

Everyone who knew Jake will miss him and those that knew him well will long for him. We will miss his wise advice, his corny jokes and his wonderful soul.

Brother

My brother was a wonderful person. Everyone he knew loved him greatly. He had an incredible sense of humor. He always came up with new ideas of how to make other people laugh. He was born five years after my parents were married, and as the first child, he was brought up with great love and attention, which made him kind of a spoiled brat.

Tell something funny your brother did.

I still remember one day when I came home and everybody was waiting for me at the dinner table. My brother asked me to sit down and eat dinner before changing my clothes as I usually did. I was a bit surprised because he had never asked me to do that.

I pulled out the chair and sat down. The moment I sat down, the sound of a fart burst out and I jumped out of the chair. Everybody burst out laughing, especially my brother who was responsible for this act. He had bought a remotely controlled electronic fart machine and taped it underneath my chair. That was just one example of his fun loving mind.

48

Now say something opposite to the funny incident to honor your brother.

At the same time, he was very caring, too. He protected me and told me that if I had a problem with anybody, just let him know and he would take care of it.

Tell about something he was good at and how he unselfishly helped you become good at it, too.

He was very caring and loving. He always knew what gift I wanted. If I asked to borrow something, he would open his closet for me. He was good at sports and won a trophy for the state championship in table tennis. He also played cricket very well and taught me how to play, which is why I am so good at them.

Tell more good things and how you feel.

He was very enthusiastic and energetic. He could solve any problem quickly. He always had time for his little brother. He taught me how to be brave, face reality and handle problems in a tactful manner. He holds a special place in my heart and his memories will remain forever in our hearts and minds.

Friend

Tell how very important your friend was to you.

John was my best friend in the world. He was the one I turned to when I thought I was in love. He was the one I turned to when I needed someone to listen. He was the one I turned to for everything.

Relate an incident where your friend was there for you.

I once called John at three in the morning to tell him about a disturbing dream I had. Once I retold my dream, he asked, "That's why you woke me up at three in the morning?" He could have hung up if he wanted to, but he didn't; he listened patiently and then made fun of me afterwards. He cared deeply for you but he also reminded you not to take yourself too seriously.

Tell about obstacles your friend overcame.

John overcame many obstacles to get where he was. In his late teens and early twenties, he realized he was an alcoholic. He told me one morning he woke up not knowing where he was, and not being able to remember the events of the past few days because he had been drinking so heavily. John told me this was when he knew that something had to change. He was able to recover from his alcoholism and lead a happy life. This was just one example of how John would meet any challenge head on, and without hesitation.

He was one of the most courageous people that I have ever met. He also was not afraid to admit when he had made mistakes. He would be the first to apologize for anything he did wrong. This was one of the qualities I admired in John.

Talk directly to your friend's spouse and tell her how you feel and how he/she can depend upon you for help.

To Mary, John's wife and his children Bobby, Sue and Dave, I promise to never forget John and always keep him in my heart. Mary, I understand why you fell in love with this man who was such a loving husband and father. We will all miss him greatly. I remember the look of pride on his face whenever he talked about his family. I am sure you know this, but he would want me to tell you again just how much he loves you. Just remember that he can he live on through our actions and words so that we may share his spirit with others. We love you, John and we miss you.

Friend

Tell how important your friend was to you.

Eleanor was one of a kind. To others, she might have seemed like a crazy girl because she was straightforward. She would not hesitate to speak up if someone did something wrong.

As far as I am concerned she was the best friend I ever had. She was the only person outside of my family I ever fully trusted. She was the person I always counted on to share my innermost secrets. She knew everything about me and I knew everything about her. There were no secrets between us. She is a part of me and holds a special place in my heart.

Tell how much fun it was being her friend and give a glimpse into what it was like.

We always enjoy each other's company. When she came to my home to spend the day, I would beg her to stay and she would end up staying for several days. I would talk her ear off and tell her every little thing that had happened since the last time we visited. She patiently listened to everything and laughed at my silly jokes.

Tell something about the old days.

I still remember those days we spent together sharing a dorm room. As her roommate I knew pretty much everything that she did. We used to chat and watch movies until four or five in the morning and then sleep late into the afternoon.

One thing that amazed me was when everybody was asleep, she would come out with a guitar in her hand and sit in the hallway and play all night. She was an excellent player and musician, and she taught herself to play. People from all over campus came to our room and begged her to play a song for them. She would not play until she made sure I wasn't studying.

Tell how special your relationship was.

We had a very good understanding of each other, which was sometimes the reason other people were envious of us. People weren't sure how we were able to get along so well and be such good friends. We never gave that secret up.

Pledge your love and support to her family.

Now, it is hard for me to believe my best friend is no longer with us. Eleanor's husband Jason

and their two children need our love and
support more than ever. And it is our duty to
Eleanor to help them through this terrible time.
Though she is no longer with us, her soul will
always remain alive.

Husband

Tell of your deep love for your husband and how he made you feel.

My husband Joe was the love of my life. I treasure the years we spent together and will always remember the warm, safe feeling I had when waking up next to him.

Tell how you met.

I first met Joe in English class when we were juniors in college. He just sat next to me and introduced himself. Somewhere along the way, we became friends during our note swapping and long study sessions. And, then on the last day of class he asked me out on a date. I said yes and the rest was history.

Talk about the wonderful way he treated you and your family.

I knew that marrying Joe was one of the best decisions I ever made. He gave me the gift of three beautiful children. Joe adored all three of our children and was a doting father. He was always trying to plan for their future and doing whatever he could to improve their lives. He worked incredibly hard to provide for our material needs, and he was never too tired to fulfill our emotional needs. I know that Don, Chris and Patty will miss his love and guidance.

Tell some of his habits and traits that made him so endearing.

Joe was not only my husband; he was my best friend. He had the ability to always make people laugh. He was infamous for telling stories about his childhood. We could always tell when he was about to tell one because he would put his hand on chin and get a dreamy look in his eyes. Often the kids would beg him to stop because they had heard them so many times. Now we all wish we could hear just one more story. Joe loved to make other people happy and he succeeded.

Express the fact that words can't really express how you feel.

This is eulogy is my tribute to my Joe and the great man he was. I know I can't express how much happiness he brought to our entire family, but if he's listening, he should know just how special he is. We love him dearly and will keep him in our hearts forever.

Wife

Talk directly to your wife.

My wife was the most beautiful and intelligent woman I ever met...that is why I married her. When we married, I knew it was forever. On that day we promised each other 'till death do us part, and so it has come to pass. Susan, I hope I have cared for you, loved you and made you happy like you deserve. Though I never pictured us apart, I know our time together here on earth is over.

Tell about how you met and how you asked her to marry you. *Note:* There is room for some humor here.

I first met Susan when we were working at the same bank together almost thirty years ago. I was the new employee and she was supposed to 'show me the ropes and help me adjust to the bank. While she was showing me around the bank and introducing me to co-workers, I just fell in love with her. I was completely distracted by her beauty and, needless to say, I was soon fired from the bank for my incompetence.

I told Susan that since it was technically her

fault that I was fired, she should at least go on a date with me. She reluctantly agreed. We got married three months later.

If applicable, talk about what it was like to have children with her or about what great she took care of you.

Susan and I have two wonderful children, Matt and Laura. Though we were both pretty nervous when Matt was born, being a mother just seemed to come naturally to Susan. She knew exactly when he needed something. She was an excellent mother.

Recap many of her best qualities.

She was also a wonderful wife and friend. She was never too busy or tired to listen to you tell about your day. She was always there for everyone and understood that it took time and effort to build meaningful relationships.

Judging from the relationships she created, it is obvious that she invested lots of her time and effort into the people she loved so dearly. I treasure the years we spent together and I know she will always be with us in our hearts.

Grandmother

Talk about how your grandparent treated you.

My grandmother would be pleasantly surprised if she could see us all gathered here today to pay tribute to her. I distinctly remember my mother arguing with my grandmother about how much she was spoiling me. But no matter what my mother said my grandmother insisted that we were hers to spoil. She always said I waited my whole life to see grandchildren and now I can finally spoil them! I heard her say one time, "If I'd known how much fun grandchildren were, I would have had them first." (Pause for laughter)

Talk about the stories she used to tell.

She insisted on only the best for us, her precious grandchildren. This was her way of showing her love and care for us. She would entertain us for hours with stories of her life as a young girl. Her tales of romance and adventure fascinated us. We pictured her as a beautiful young woman with many suitors, who instead of getting married at an early age as tradition dictated, set out on her own.

Talk about her history.

She headed to the big city of New York and tried her luck as a secretary. There she met our grandfather who was the mailman. Very soon after they met they were married.

Tell things you learned from her.

My grandmother challenged conformity, refusing to live her life according to what everyone else thought was right. She was a forward thinking woman. I strive to be like her.

Though we did not know the hardships she endured until we ourselves grew up, we always appreciated her strength. We spent all of our summers at Grandma's house. It was during those summers that we learned more valuable information than we learned throughout the whole school year. We learned how to be independent thinkers and make daring moves. And, most importantly, she taught us to love each other.

We will miss Grandma's sharp wit, her exciting stories and most of all her tender love for everyone.

Grandfather

Tell how much you revere your grandfather.
My grandfather was one of the greatest people that I know. He was the kind of grandfather that everyone wanted, the kind of mentor that everyone wished they had and the kind of person people were honored to know.

Talk about your childhood memories of your grandfather.

Ever since I could remember, a visit from my grandfather meant lots of candy and games. We played everything from Scrabble and Chutes and Ladders to Hungry Hippos. Grandpa Lou always said you are as old as you feel. He always told us that we, his grandchildren kept him young. We would play kickball, softball and basketball out in the yard. Grandpa was always up for anything. He never let anyone tell him what to do or what not to do. He lived his life the way that he wanted. His fierce stubbornness could at times work to our advantage. It was helpful when he convinced our mother that she should let us stay up past our bedtime, but not when he made us go to school.

Talk about his great character and any awards he had.

I know it was hard for grandfather when grandmother died, but he showed us how courageous he was and went on with his life. He did not simply teach us values and morals but he taught them by example. He lived his life by the same values that he instilled in us. People like that are rare today. He used to tell us that he learned most of what he knew about anything while he was in the Navy. He learned hard work, discipline, loyalty and love. He dedicated himself to whatever assignment he was given. A captain once wrote a letter of recommendation for my grandfather and said; "Every once in a while you meet a young man who stands out and displays wisdom and courage beyond his years, and Lou is exactly that young man."

These are just some of my memories of my grandfather. I will always remember his big bear hugs, his booming laughter and his warm smile.

Seize the moment. Remember all those women on the Titanic who waved off the dessert cart.

--Erma Bombeck,
American Humorist

Chapter 3

Planning a Funeral

In addition to writing a eulogy, you may be making funeral arrangements for your loved one. This is a difficult process requiring some research and careful planning.

Consider questions while arranging the funeral:

- ✓ How do I select a funeral home?
- ✓ What are different ways to arrange the body?
- ✓ How do I obtain a death certificate?
- ✓ How do I notify other family and friends?
- ✓ How can I buy a cemetery plot?

- ✓ Which casket do I select?
- ✓ What if I am on a budget?
- ✓ Is there a life insurance plan or funeral insurance with money already set aside?

And most importantly...

- ✓ How do I keep my sanity?
- ✓ How do I make sure I'm getting my money's worth?

All of these questions may seem overwhelming, but answering each of them will help you plan a proper funeral.

First, there are several options for taking care of the body after death. It can be buried, entombed, cremated or even given to a medical school. It is up to you and your family to decide which process you want. Depending on the wishes of the deceased, the family, or religious beliefs, you should decide what is going to actually happen to the body.

Finding a funeral home

The best way to start looking for a funeral home

is to just open up the phone book or search on the Internet and start calling places in your area. Decide what your price range is and work within these boundaries. Contact the lawyer or accountant of the deceased to find out if there was any funeral or life insurance that might help pay for the arrangements. There may be money set aside to help cover the expenses of the ceremony.

Funeral homes are required to give estimates over the telephone so make sure you get these. Ask for an estimate over the phone, and then if it is reasonable, go there in person and speak with the funeral home director. Once you have decided which funeral home to use, go there in person and work out estimates on paper.

Before signing any contracts or agreeing to any payments, be sure you are absolutely clear about what has been discussed. Realize that there are also alternatives to having the funeral in a funeral home. Many have been held in homes, parks or other special places.

What should you do if you feel that you cannot handle making these arrangements and are too distraught? Then you might want to consider asking a close friend or relative to help you with

these duties. Choose someone who is aware of any financial limits and who is trustworthy.
Ask yourself some key questions:

- ✓ Does this person understand your goals for the funeral?

- ✓ Would they be able to speak to the funeral director on your behalf?

- ✓ Do you trust them?

- ✓ Will they be willing to take on these responsibilities?

Caskets

If you decide that you want to bury your loved one, you must decide on a casket. The funeral home will most likely offer you a casket. However, you may want to look into buying the casket from a casket retailer. These retailers will often offer you better prices. Be aware that you are not obligated to buy a casket from the funeral home!

The two principal caskets to choose from are metal and wood. There are several types of wood. Depending on the quality and availability of the wood used, the price of the casket will vary.

There also many types of metal caskets which differ in price based on the type of metal used. It is up to you and your family to decide the type of casket you prefer. If you are on a budget, the lowest priced wood casket will be made of pine and the lowest priced metal casket will be made of steel.

Steel caskets come in a variety of gauges or thicknesses of the metal. The higher the number, the thinner the steel and the cheaper the casket. I.e., everything else being equal, a 20 gauge casket should be cheaper than a 18 gauge or a 16 gauge casket which would be the most expensive of the three.

Other metal caskets are made of copper or bronze, both of which are impervious to rust. Bronze is considered a semi-precious metal and is the most expensive of the metal caskets.

Wood caskets come in mahogany, walnut, cherry, maple, oak, pecan, birch, poplar, and pine and are generally priced according to the value of the wood.

Other factors that affect the price are the interior quality and the finish of the corners and the overall finish of the casket.

There are also "sealed" caskets, which some reports say cause the bodies to swell up. Though sealed caskets are often recommended and are more expensive, they **do not** necessarily provide better protection for the corpse.

Embalming

Some states do not require embalming, so specify whether or not you would like the body embalmed. Embalming gives the tissue a life like appearance for a short time and is necessary if you are having an open casket viewing at the funeral or if the body must be transported on open carrier. There are several specific circumstances the Federal Trade Commission spells out when embalming is necessary. If the funeral home embalms the body and charges for it, they must explain why in writing.

Also, if you decide to have a viewing ceremony, you may want to consider having floral arrangements for the casket. Though this is optional, it adds a nice touch to the ceremony. There are florists that offer special bouquets or baskets. Keep in mind that these items can be quite highly priced. If you are looking for a lower priced alternative, grocery stores and local floral shops may offer similar flower packages at a lower price.

Cemeteries

If you are looking for a cemetery plot, contact local cemeteries and arrange a meeting with them. Look for cemeteries that are well cared for. Ask what exactly is done and how often the cemetery is maintained. Ask about their visitation policy and about placing flowers on the grave.

Some cemeteries may charge you for a grave liner, which prevents the graves from sinking in. There are many types of headstones including flat or rounded ones. Think about the type of headstone you want and the epitaph that will be engraved on the headstone.

You may compose the epitaph. Epitaphs can be traditional, they can be poems, or they can be humorous. A person may have specified exactly what they wanted on their headstone, so be sure to check this before writing an epitaph. Type the word "epitaph" into any major search engine and you will find many examples.

Your Rights as a Consumer

As a consumer you should know your rights regarding funerals.
There are several laws that funeral homes and funeral home directors are required to follow. You may want to familiarize yourself with these to be sure you are getting what you deserve. The Federal Trade Commission regulates the funeral industry and sets all their laws. See http://www.ftc.gov/bcp/rulemaking/funeral/

Notification

When notifying family and friends, you may choose to send letters, e-mails, make telephone calls or even send death notifications. Choose the option with which you are the most comfortable.

You may also want to consider publishing an obituary in the local newspaper. Though this will cost more, it is one way to notify other people. Just call the paper where you would like it to be published and ask how to go about getting an obituary.

Some families like to suggest donations to

charities or trust funds in the name of the deceased. One way to collect the money for this is at the funeral or by mail. Simple cards may be sent out requesting that people donate to a specific charity in the person's name.

Gatherings

Funerals are often followed by a wake or gathering. These can be held at homes, parks or any special location. Minimize expenses by making or providing snacks and refreshments at home rather than through a caterer. Most of the time friends and family members will volunteer to bring food or help at such an event. The purpose of this gathering is to get together and reminisce about memories of the deceased. It can be seen as a celebration of their life rather than a time to mourn their loss.

Death Certificate

The death certificate simply contains vital information such as name, date of birth and date of death, etc. You must obtain an official death certificate. Either go directly to a state government office to do this or search online for companies that can perform this task.

If you obtain the certificate from the state government, be aware that different states have different requirements. You just have to specifically ask what must be done to get the official death certificate.

It is a good idea to get several original death certificates because insurance companies, trusts, and many other places may require an original document.

These links can help you with the instructions for your state:
http://www.vitalrec.com/death.html

http://www.cdc.gov/nchs/howto/w2w/w2welcom.htm

Shop around and be wary

The best way to be sure that you get your money's worth is to ask questions, shop around, know what you want and know your rights!

Though you may be too upset to shop around, remember not to equate the price with how much you loved the person. Spending less money doesn't mean you loved that person less! It might sound awful, but you are dealing with people in a business and they are not always honest and may try to take advantage of you. Since you are vulnerable, be wary and careful of what people tell you and make sure all charges are legitimate and accurate.

Chapter 4

Resources

Grieving is a difficult time in your life. Several support groups can help you cope with your loss. Here are a few links where you may find other people in a similar situation

Grief Support

www.counselingforloss.com
www.griefnet.org
www.compassionatefriends.org
www.groww.org
www.griefshare.org
www.growingthroughgrief.com
www.bereavement.net
www.grieflossrecovery.com

www.grief-recovery.com
www.griefcounselors.com
www.centerforloss.com
www.atimetogrieve.net
www.healinghearts.net

Funeral Planning Resources

For Funeral Planning:
www.funeral.com
www.funeralplan.com
www.funerals.org
www.funerals-ripoffs.org
www.funeraldepot.com
www.burialitems.com
www.classicmemorials.com
www.funeralnet.com
www.thefuneraldirectory.com
www.finalplans.com

For Flowers:
www.funeralflowers.com
www.1stinfuneralflowers.com
www.24hrfuneralflowers.com
www.funeralflowersdirect.com
www.funeral-flowers.net

Exploring some of these sites might help answer questions and help you locate funeral homes and services near you. If you have time, it is strongly recommended to search through some of these websites to get an idea of how to go about doing certain things. These sights cater to people in the same situation as you and have answers to many questions and may guide you to more resources.

*God's finger touched him
and he slept.*

--Lord Alfred Tennyson

Chapter 5

Checklists

Initial Steps Checklist

Here are some initial steps to take after you have learned of someone's death:

- ✓ Find out where the body is. It may already in a morgue or need to be transported to a funeral home.
- ✓
- ✓ Be sure to specify whether or not you want the body to be embalmed.

✓ To see if there is a will, contact the person's lawyer and check where the deceased kept important documents, such as in a safety deposit box at a bank.

✓ Check the will for any specific burial instructions and for insurance policies. These insurance policies may help pay for the funeral expenses or you may cash the life insurance to pay for the funeral.

✓ In order to cash any of these policies you will need an official death certificate. These can be obtained by contacting the State Coroner. The time that it takes to get these certificates varies from state to state.

✓ Decide what kind of ceremony will be performed. There are several options including burial, cremation and entombment.

✓ If you have no money to pay for a funeral
   or no way of even getting any money,
   then one solution is to give the body to a
   medical school to be used for research.
   Then you can hold a memorial service
   without the actual body being present.

✓ Funerals can cost thousands of dollars!
   Be careful what you spend your money on
   and be sure each expense is valid.

✓ Decide on a funeral home. Select a casket.
   And arrange for a vehicle to carry the
   body to be carried from the funeral home
   to the cemetery.

✓ If there will just be a memorial service,
   fix a location and notify those who need
   to know. You can notify them by sending
   cards, either letters, e-mails or even
   making telephone calls.

Decision Checklist

Here are a few questions to ask when selecting a method to dispose of the body and choosing an container for the body:

- ✓ Are there any religious rules or customs that dictate what to do with the body?

- ✓ What method does the family prefer?

- ✓ Did the deceased leave any specific instructions of what was to be done?

- ✓ What is my budget?

- ✓ How is the funeral going to be paid for?

- ✓ Would you prefer a metal or a wood casket?

- ✓ If there is going to be a burial, which cemetery will they be placed in? Did you choose a cemetery plot?

✓ If there is a cremation, what will happen to the ashes? Will they be put in an urn or scattered in nature?

✓ If they are placed in a mausoleum, in which vault or crypt will they be?

✓ Do you want the funeral to be in a funeral home or in a park, home or other location?

Pre-Funeral Checklist

Here is a checklist of tasks that should be taken care of before the actual funeral:

✓ Arrange for flowers to be on the casket and in the funeral home.

✓ If there is a viewing, specify how you want the body to be placed.

✓ Decide the seating arrangement.

✓ Select an outfit for the deceased person.

✓ Plan the sequence of events for the funeral (i.e. when the eulogy should be given).

✓ Make arrangements for the body to be transported from the funeral home to the graveyard.

✓ If there will be a funeral procession with everyone following the hearse in their cars, then make signs indicating you are all traveling together (The funeral home may take care of this).

✓ Arrange for flowers to be at the burial site.

✓ Select the pallbearers who will carry the casket.

✓ Have cards sent out indicating where and when the funeral will take place.

Funeral Home Checklist

Here are some things to consider when dealing with the funeral home and funeral director:

✓ Talk to several different funeral homes and see which one is best for you.

✓ Did you work out an estimate on paper of the expenses?

✓ Keep in mind that you do not have to use the casket provided by the funeral home.

✓ Ask if you can talk to other customers and see if they had a satisfactory experience with the funeral home.

✓ Find out the maximum capacity of people in the funeral home.

✓ Make sure to go over specific items like transporting the body to the funeral home and to the final resting place.

Chapter 6

Serious Quotations

I believe that imagination is stronger than knowledge, that myth is more potent than history. I believe that dreams are more powerful than facts, that hope always triumphs over experience, that laughter is the only cure for grief. And I believe that love is stronger than death.
— From the movie The Crow

When I look back on all these worries, I remember the story of the old man who said on his deathbed that he had had a lot of trouble in his life, most of which had never happened.
— Winston Churchill

We all labor against our own cure, for death is the cure of all diseases.
— Unknown

If I think more about death than some other people, it is probably because I love life more than they do.
— Angelina Jolie

The mystery of love is greater than the mystery of death.
— Unknown

There will always be death and taxes; however, death doesn't get worse every year.
— Unknown

A single death is a tragedy; a million deaths is a statistic.
— Joseph Stalin

We cast away priceless time in dreams, born of imagination, fed upon illusion, and put to death by reality.
— Judy Garland

Never chase a lie. Let it alone, and it will run itself to death.
— Lyman Beecher

There is no goal better than this one: to know as you lie on your deathbed that you lived your true life, and you did whatever made you happy.
– Steve Chandler

Love never dies a natural death. It dies because we don't know how to replenish its source. It dies of blindness and errors and betrayals. It dies of illness and wounds; it dies of weariness, of witherings, of tarnishings.
– Unknown

Death ends a life, not a relationship.
– Jack Lemmon

We must love one another or die.
– W.H. Auden

Nothing in life is certain except death and taxes.
– Benjamin Franklin

Life is pleasant. Death is peaceful. It's the transition that's troublesome
– Isaac Asimov

I know not what course others may take, but as for me, give me liberty or give me death.
– Patrick Henry

A man's ethical behavior should be based effectually on sympathy, education, and social ties; no religious basis is necessary. Man would indeed be in a poor way if he had to be restrained by fear of punishment and hope of reward after death.
                    – Albert Einstein

The silence that guards the tomb does not reveal God's secret in the obscurity of the coffin, and the rustling of the branches whose roots suck the body's elements do not tell the mysteries of the grave, by the agonized sighs of my heart announce to the living the drama which love, beauty, and death have performed.
     – Kahlil Gibran, Broken Wings

It's not catastrophes, murders, deaths, diseases, that age and kill us; it's the way people look and laugh, and run up the steps of omnibuses.
               – Virginia Woolf

Men fear death, as children fear to go in the dark; and as that natural fear in children is increased with tales, so is the other.
             – Francis Bacon

Born Free...'taxed to Death
                 – Unknown

92

Life is eternal and love is immortal; and death is only a horizon, and a horizon is nothing save the limit of our sight.
>   – Rossiter W. Raymond

Love the man that can smile in trouble, that can gather strength from distress, and grow brave by reflection. 'Tis the business of little minds to shrink, but he whose heart is firm, and whose conscience approves his conduct, will pursue his principles unto death.
>   – Thomas Paine

If man hasn't discovered something that he will die for, he isn't fit to live
>   – Martin Luther King

He is one of those people who would be enormously improved by death
>   – H.H. Munroe

Why do we kill people who are killing people to show that killing people is wrong?
>   – Holly Near

For death is no more than a turning of us over from time to eternity.
>   – William Penn

To be idle is a short road to death and to be diligent is a way of life; foolish people are idle, wise people are diligent.
> – Buddha (B.C.E. 568-488)

Every man dies. Not every man really lives.
> – William Wallace

What we have done for ourselves alone dies with us; what we have done for others and the world remains and is immortal.
> – Albert Pike

For death is no more than a turning of us over from time to eternity.
> – William Penn

For what is it to die, but to stand in the sun and melt into the wind? And when the Earth has claimed our limbs, then we shall truly dance.
> – Kahlil Gibran

The day which we fear as our last is but the birthday of eternity.
> – Seneca

A man is not completely born until he is dead.
> – Benjamin Franklin

Death is not extinguishing the light; it is putting out the lamp because dawn has come.
— Rabindranath Tagore

While we are mourning the loss of our friend, others are rejoicing to meet him behind the veil.
— John Taylor

Only nature has a right to grieve perpetually, for she only is innocent. Soon the ice will melt, and the blackbirds sing along the river, which he frequented, as pleasantly as ever. The same everlasting serenity will appear in this face of God, and we will not be sorrowful, if he is not
— Henry David Thoreau
(upon the death of his brother)

What we commonly call death does not destroy the body; it only causes a separation of spirit and body.
— Brigham Young

While we are mourning the loss of our friend, others are rejoicing to meet him behind the veil.
— John Taylor

Is death the last sleep? No · it is the last and final awakening.
— Sir Walter Scott

Be of good cheer about death and know this as a truth – that no evil can happen to a good man, either in life or after death.
> – Socrates

We sometimes congratulate ourselves at the moment of waking from a troubled dream...it may be so at the moment of death.
> – Nathaniel Hawthorne

Each departed friend is a magnet that attracts us to the next world.
> – Jean Paul Richter

Nothing can happen more beautiful than death.
> – Walt Whitman

Death is the most beautiful adventure in life.
> – Charles Frohman

Life is eternal and love is immortal; and death is only a horizon, and a horizon is nothing, save the limit of our sight.
> – Rossiter W. Raymond

Neither fire nor wind, birth nor death can erase our good deeds.
> – Buddha (B.C.E. 568-488)

For in that sleep of death, what dreams may come.
> – William Shakespeare, Hamlet

I said to Life, "I would hear Death speak." And Life raised her voice a little higher and said, "You hear him now."
> – Kahlil Gibran

Birth and Death are the two noblest expressions of bravery.
> – Kahlil Gibran

Desire is half of life, indifference is half of death.
> – Kahlil Gibran

To be idle is a short road to death and to be diligent is a way of life; foolish people are idle, wise people are diligent.
> – Buddha (B.C.E. 568-488)

Neither fire nor wind, birth nor death can erase our good deeds.
> – Buddha (B.C.E. 568-488)

I shall not die of a cold. I shall die of having lived.
> – Willa Cather

Even at our birth, death does but stand aside a little. And every day he looks towards us and muses somewhat to himself whether that day or the next he will draw nigh.
— Robert Bolt

Our fear of death is like our fear that summer will be short, but when we have had our swing of pleasure, our fill of fruit, and our swelter of heat, we say we have had our day.
— Ralph Waldo Emerson

They that sow in tears shall reap in joy.
— Psalms

To be idle is a short road to death and to be diligent is a way of life; foolish people are idle, wise people are diligent.
— Buddha (B.C.E. 568-488)

I have died many a death in love, and yet, had I not loved I would never have lived at all.
— David Lasater

Anything I've ever done that ultimately was worthwhile... initially scared me to death.
— Betty Bender

The great Easter truth is not that we are to live newly after death – that is not the great thing – but that...we are to, and may, live nobly now because we are to live forever.
– Phillips Brooks

If Easter says anything to us today, it says this: You can put truth in a grave, but it won't stay there. You can nail it to a cross, wrap it in winding sheets and shut it up in a tomb, but it will rise!
– Clarence W. Hall

To be idle is a short road to death and to be diligent is a way of life; foolish people are idle, wise people are diligent.
– Buddha (B.C.E. 568-488)

There are two types of education... One should teach us how to make a living, and the other how to live.
– John Adams

I would rather live and love where death is king than have eternal life where love is not.
– Robert G. Ingersoll

Love is life and if you miss love, you miss life.
– Leo Buscaglia

To infinite, ever present Love, all is Love, and there is no error, no sin, sickness nor death.
— Mary Baker Eddy

Without an understanding of myth or religion, without an understanding of the relationship between destruction and creation, death and rebirth, the individual suffers the mysteries of life as meaningless mayhem alone.
— Marion Woodman, Canadian analyst, writer

Ancient Egyptians believed that upon death they would be asked two questions and their answers would determine whether they could continue their journey in the afterlife. The first question was, "Did you bring joy?" The second was, "Did you find joy?"
— Leo Buscaglia

For life in the present there is no death. Death is not an event in life. It is not a fact in the world.
— Wittgenstein

Death borders upon our birth, and our cradle stands in the grave. Our birth is nothing but our death begun.
— Bishop Hall

Do not take thought for your persons or your properties, but first and chiefly to care about the greatest improvement of the soul. I tell you that the virtue is not given by money, but that from virtue comes money and every other good of man, public as well as private... The difficulty, my friends, is not in avoiding death, but in avoiding unrighteousness; for that runs faster than death.
— Socrates

What lies behind us and what lies before us are tiny matters compared to what lies within us.
— Ralph Waldo Emerson

We enjoy warmth because we have been cold. We appreciate light because we have been in darkness. By the same token, we can experience joy because we have known sadness.
— David Weatherford

You will never be happy if you continue to search for what happiness consists of. You will never live if you are looking for the meaning of life.
— Albert Camus

Maybe this world is another planet's hell.
— Aldous Huxley

Life seems but a quick succession of busy nothings.
> – Jane Austen

Although the world is full of suffering, it is also full of the overcoming of it.
> – Helen Keller

The walls we build around us to keep out the sadness also keep out the joy.
> – Jim Rohn

However long the night, the dawn will break.
> – African Proverb

There are as many nights as days, and the one is just as long as the other in the year's course. Even a happy life cannot be without a measure of darkness, and the word 'happy' would lose its meaning if it were not balanced by sadness.
> – Carl Jung

Life isn't about finding yourself. Life is about creating yourself.
> – George Bernard Shaw

We make a living by what we get, but we make a life by what we give.
> – Norman MacEwan

It is wonderful how much time good people spend fighting the devil. If they would only expend the same amount of energy loving their fellow men, the devil would die in his own tracks of ennui.

        – Helen Keller

Ask yourself whether the dream of heaven and greatness should be waiting for us in our graves – or whether it should be ours here and now and on this earth.

        – Ayn Rand

Begin doing what you want to do now. We are not living in eternity. We have only this moment, sparkling like a star in our hand and melting like a snowflake.

        – Marie Beyon Ray

Our lives begin to end the day we become silent about things that matter.

        – Martin Luther King, Jr.

I like living. I have sometimes been wildly, despairingly, acutely miserable, racked with sorrow, but through it all I still know quite certainly that just to be alive is a grand thing.

        – Agatha Christie

103

How far you go in life depends on your being tender with the young, compassionate with the aged, sympathetic with the striving, and tolerant of the weak and strong. Because someday in your life you will have been all of these.
— George Washington Carver

Death is a very dull, dreary affair, and my advice to you is to have nothing whatsoever to do with it.
— W. Somerset Maugham, author

We shall find peace. We shall hear the angels; we shall see the sky sparkling with diamonds.
— Anton Chekhov

God's finger touched him and he slept.
— Lord Alfred Tennyson

Death is not a period, but a comma in the story of life.
— Amos Traver

It is foolish to be afraid of death. JUST THINK!! No more repaired tires on the body vehicle, no more patchwork living.
— Paramhansa Yogananda

Do not believe in anything simply because you have heard it. Do not believe in anything simply because it is spoken and rumored by many. Do not believe in anything simply because it is found written in your religious books. Do not believe in anything merely on the authority of your teachers and elders. Do not believe in traditions because they have been handed down for many generations. But after observation and analysis, when you find that anything agrees with reason and is conducive to the good and benefit of one and all, then accept it and live up to it.

– Buddha

Tears are sometimes an inappropriate response to death. When a life has been lived completely honestly, completely successful, or just completely, the correct response to death's perfect punctuation mark is a smile.

– Julie Burchill

There are stars whose radiance is visible on earth though they have long been extinct. There are people whose brilliance continues to light the world though they are no longer among the living. These lights are particularly bright when the night is dark.

– Hannah Senesh

If I could wish for my life to be perfect, it would be tempting but I would have to decline, for life would no longer teach me anything.
　　　　　　　　– Allyson Jones

Your living is determined not so much by what life brings to you as by the attitude you bring to life; not so much by what happens to you as by the way your mind looks at what happens. Circumstances and situations do color life but you have been given the mind to choose what the color shall be.
　　　　　　　　– John Homer Miller

Everyone is a house with four rooms, a physical, a mental, an emotional and a spiritual. Most of us tend to live in one room most of the time, but unless we go into every room, every day, even if only to keep it aired, we are not a complete person.
　　　　　　　　– Indian Proverb

I have never killed a man, but I have read many obituaries with great pleasure.
　　　　　　　　– Clarence Darrow

We gather strength from sadness and from pain. Each time we die we learn to live again.
　　　　　　　　– Source Unknown

106

Life is part positive and part negative. Suppose you went to hear a symphony orchestra and all they played were the little happy high notes. Would you leave soon? Let me hear the rumble of the bass, the crash of the cymbals and the minor keys.
— Jim Rohn

When the heart grieves over what it has lost, the spirit rejoices over what it has left.
— Sufi Epigram

Heaven will be inherited by every man who has heaven in his soul.
— Henry Ward Beecher

Never does one feel oneself so utterly helpless as in trying to speak comfort for great bereavement. I will not try it. Time is the only comforter for the loss of a mother.
— Jane Welsh Carlyle

If, as I can't help suspecting, the dead also feel the pains of separation (and this may be one of their purgatorial sufferings), then for both lovers, and for all pairs of lovers without exception, bereavement is a universal and integral part of our experience of love.
— C's. Lewis Humorous Quotations

In the end, everything is a gag.
> – Charlie Chaplin

I didn't attend the funeral, but I sent a nice letter saying I approved of it.
> – Mark Twain

Some men are alive simply because it is against the law to kill them.
> – Ed Howe

Death and taxes and childbirth! There's never any convenient time for any of them.
> – Margaret Mitchell (Gone With the Wind)

Seize the moment. Remember all those women on the Titanic who waved off the dessert cart.
> – Erma Bombeck, American Humorist

Good friends, good books and a sleepy conscience: this is the ideal life.
> – Mark Twain

Be happy while you're living, for you're a long time dead.
> – Scottish Proverb

Taking joy in life is a woman's best cosmetic.
> – Rosalind Russell

Red is the ultimate cure for sadness.
— Bill Blass

A time to weep, and a time to laugh; a time to mourn, and a time to dance.
— Ecclesiastes 3:4

Father Sullivan was ministering to a man on his deathbed. "Renounce Satan!" yelled Father Sullivan. "No," said the dying man. "I say, renounce the devil and his works!" "No," the man repeats. "And why, in the name of all that is holy, not?" asks Father Sullivan. "Because," said the dying man, "I want to wait until I see where I'm heading before I start annoying anybody."

We sincerely wish the best for you
in the face of your loss.

Begin doing what you want to do now. We are not living in eternity. We have only this moment, sparkling like a star in our hand and melting like a snowflake.

--Marie Beyon Ray

Chapter 7

A Special Bonus

As a special bonus, we are sharing the tribute Tom Antion, international public speaker and Internet marketer, wrote as a special memorial to his dad, Sam Antion. Tom says, "The document you write will probably be saved and handed down from generation to generation in your family." As you read the following, think about how you can use Tom's technique to capture the legacy of your loved one for future generations.

This bonus section is as near to my heart as you can get. What you will be seeing is a reprint of my Internet Magazine's annual memorial issue to my father. It came about when I returned home after doing his eulogy.

"Great Speaking" is the largest Internet magazine in the world for professional level public speaking. After I got back from dad's funeral it was just about time to put out a new issue and I just didn't feel like it. I took a look at my notes from the eulogy I had just delivered and promptly started crying. I was faced with the work of putting out my magazine, but just couldn't get my dad and all he had taught me out of my mind.

What you see below is an unedited outpouring of my love for my dad that just came out. I don't remember too well writing it, but I guess I did because it went out in my magazine and I got email from hundreds of people around the world telling me how this issue touched them. Many went on to write similar things for their parents both living and dead.

It turns out that I stumbled upon an idea that could just work wonders for you and the document you write will probably be saved and handed down from generation to generation in your family.

David Letterman probably wouldn't get too many laughs with this one, but the idea is basically a top ten list of things I learned from my dad. Of course, since I publish a magazine for speakers I related what I had done to the public speaking arena.

This issue is quite a bit different from our usual fare of speaking tips. This issue is a special memorial issue to my dad and it has its own special lesson that I hope you can use in your speeches.

Leadership Skills from a Man Who Came to America in a Dung Filled Cattle Boat
In memory of Sam Antion
March 27, 1907 - July 2, 2000

(Reprint of the July 7, 2000 memorial issue of Great Speaking. Ezine)

Note from Tom: Well, another year has gone by and this is the anniversary of my dad's death. You can expect to see this issue as long as I'm publishing every year on July 2. This is also a chance for Dad to touch 100,000 more people since that's how much "Great Speaking" has grown since last July.

I'm hoping that you parents out there ask yourselves the following question after you read the ten leadership life tips my dad gave me:

"What would my children say about me if they were writing this?"

For those of you out there that did not have good parents and those of you that even hate your parents, I hope you get something out of this too. I was fortunate. Maybe you were not. I'm hoping that you break the chain in your family and do whatever it takes so that your children will feel as strongly about you as I still do about my dad.

I've been bragging about my dad ever since 1973 when I did my graduation speech. I've even done professional speeches about one of the techniques he used to make me tough when I was just a baby (see below). Until I was preparing his eulogy this past week, I have never actually written down all the leadership skills he taught me. As I was working on them, I thought that they would be a good example that anyone could use both in their life and from the platform.

I only saw dad speak in public once and that was at his 50th wedding anniversary, but I witnessed the leadership skills listed below, my whole life

Dad's Memorial Top 10 List:

LEADERSHIP SKILL 1
Build it strong

Dad would always build things more sturdy than they needed to be so that he would never have to worry when an extraordinary force was applied. He knew that whatever he built would stand up to the test. This applied to both character traits and real hammer and nail construction.

In fact, without his insistence on this leadership trait, I would not be here today.

When I was 16 years old a drunk driver doing nearly 100 mph (161 kph) ran his car off the road smashing it into the corner of our living room. I was the only one in the room when it exploded around me. Had this been a normally built house the car would have burst thru the wall and killed me.

LEADERSHIP SKILL 2
Don't take short cuts

Dad was an electrician by trade. When doing his wiring he would always route the flat wires he worked with in a nice symmetrical and evenly spaced pattern. He would never just cut across the shortest distance to save wire and make his costs a little cheaper. I remember as a child watching him and asking him why he did this when it would be a lot shorter to just run the wires directly between two points. He said,

"When someone looks at this job years from now they will know that a professional did it and also, if they ever have trouble, they will be able to track down the problem easier because I did a nice neat job."

I can't remember dad ever being out of work one day in my whole life. When everyone else was laid-off, he was always in demand.

LEADERSHIP SKILL 3
Don't waste things or people

Think a rock isn't worth much? Read on. At the age of 73, dad was purchasing some used lumber that someone had advertised in the paper. When he went to pick it up, he saw a large number of boulders in the front yard of the place where he bought the lumber. He asked what they were going to do with the boulders. The man said, "I just want to get them out of here." Dad spent two weeks hauling them back to our house and another two months cutting them up with a chisel and a hammer. He then built a beautiful stone fireplace and chimney for one of our rental properties.

Also, I can't tell you the number of nails I

removed from used lumber Dad made me straighten and use over again. I still do it to this day. A bent nail with a little help can be very useful again. Sometimes people also need a little help to do the job they were meant to do.

LEADERSHIP SKILL 4
Be self reliant

Working as a team is great, but when the team isn't there you just don't sit down and wait for help. Dad built pretty much every building and rental property we own. I remember being so busy with football and other activities that I didn't get to help him too much (I probably would have slowed him down anyway). One day while he was working on remodeling one of our buildings he asked me to go to the automotive parts store to get him about 20 feet of clear gas line tubing and several bottles of Coca Cola. I wondered what he was up to because he never drank Coke and our car was working fine.

I came back with the tubing and the Coke and stood back and watched as he did his thing. He plugged one end of the tubing and started pouring Coke in the other end (I was sure he had lost his mind after spending three months building the chimney). He said, "When you boys aren't around it's hard for me to make things level because I can't be at both ends of these long 2x4s. So I'm going to nail one end of this tubing on one end of where I'm working and take the other end of the tubing with me to the other end of the board. He knew from his self-taught physics studies that liquids seek their own level. He could see through the clear tubing to the Coca Cola inside. The level of the Coke on one end of the tubing would be exactly the same level as at the other end of the tubing and that's where he would nail his board and it was always perfectly level.

LEADERSHIP SKILL 5
Study

Dad only went to the 5th grade and that was after skipping two grades, so he really only had three years of formal education. At ten years old (the oldest boy with father deceased) he was head of his household and shining shoes to support the family. He saved part of his tips and ordered an electrical engineering course from the American School. At 13 he had his own electrical contracting company and installed the first electric light in Carnegie, PA. He also bought his younger sister the first electric washing tub in Bridgeville, PA

He would read, read, and read some more every time he wanted to learn how to do something. When he retired around the age of 73 he sat down and read the ENTIRE World Book Encyclopedia. Now that's a lot of reading! Still at 94 and being legally blind he listened to hours and hours of biographies and books on tape, and newspapers on tape provided by the Library of Congress for blind people. He knew more about current events than anyone. If you want to learn how to do something, study and try it out until you get it right.

LEADERSHIP SKILL 6
You can have whatever you want if you are willing to work for it

This was the 1910 version of "Just do it." I don't want you to think I wasn't given tons of things by my parents, because I was. But the most valuable thing was that I was conditioned from a very young age that the world didn't "owe" me a living. I had to earn it. I got a serious work ethic that I will always carry with me. If I want something, I go after it. I won't step on people to get whatever it is, and I won't cheat or steal, but I will work until I get it or don't want it anymore. This would be a foreign language to many of today's youth.

LEADERSHIP SKILL 7
Give before you get

During the depression, work was more than scarce...more like nonexistent. Even my dad was out of work. He told me that he said to himself, "I'm a really valuable worker and I'm not going to sit around here and do nothing when there is work out there to be done." He knew there was a fruit shipping warehouse not too far from where he lived so he went down to the loading docks dressed for work and just started helping the men load apples. Eventually the foreman noticed him and asked the other guys who he was. They said they didn't know but that he just started loading apples. In fact, he was doing the work of three men. The foreman was so impressed he hired him on the spot and he hired several of my dad's cousins who were willing to prove themselves first.

Not realizing I was being influenced by my dad, I used to do the same thing when my landlord in college would work on our house. I would go out and help him just to learn how to fix things. This same landlord gave me the biggest financial break of my young career when he guaranteed the financing and sold me his largest rental property when he retired to Florida and I hadn't even graduated from college yet.

LEADERSHIP SKILL 8
You can overcome obstacles

This is one of my favorites. I have a visual that I use in a segment of a program called "You are Unstoppable."
The visual depicts a baby crawling on cushions with a red ball on the other side of the cushions.
http://www.antion.com

Dad told me that he would put my toys on one side of the room and put pillows in front of me to teach me to overcome obstacles. Anyone that knows me sees all the time that I'll figure a way to get something done if it is worthwhile getting done.

Knowing that you can't be held back no matter what happens to you is a very powerful feeling to have inside. It gives you an unbridled confidence. Both my parents aligned to make me feel this way. Most of you don't know this about me, but 14 years ago I lost everything and was totally broke, sleeping on a mattress in a vacant house, injured and unable to walk, and living off credit cards. The powerful feeling burned inside of me to overcome this obstacle which I did by coming up with an idea for a unique entertainment company that in turn helped launch my speaking career.

LEADERSHIP SKILL 9
Stick by your spouse

(Well I haven't had much chance to try this one out yet, but when I do get the chance, I will. :) My dad stuck by my mother even when, as a know-it-all teenager, I knew she was clearly wrong. Maybe that's why they made it 57 +years. (I'll have more to say on this one if I ever get some real life experience. ha ha ha ha)

LEADERSHIP SKILL 10
Risk everything for something really worthwhile

Did you ever wonder why many people don't achieve their goals? Could it be because they were never really willing to commit fully to them? ... They always gave themselves easy outs so if the going got tough they could bail out easily. Around 1946 with a house full of kids and more on the way, Dad took every nickel he had, went 50 miles out of the city and bought 156 acres of land, a bull dozer and enough fuel to run it. He did not want his kids being raised in the filthy air and tough streets of Pittsburgh, PA. He built a truck stop and motel and eventually warehouses, rental cottages and our house on National Route 40 one mile east of Claysville, PA His work can still be seen there today (along with the chimney I mentioned earlier that is on one of our rental properties).

All the kids grew up healthy and strong and not one ever got into any trouble (except the time I ran away from home and ate grass soup and hotdogs for two hours before I gave up and returned home)

Well even though Dad was only on stage once that I know of, his leadership principles are influencing tens of thousands of people through me and because of all the people he touched over the years. I spent the 4th of July this week at the funeral home viewing which, to be honest, I thought was going to be a pretty barren site ...especially at his age because all his friends had died off... I couldn't believe it... People were everywhere. People that I'd never seen before or even heard of were telling me stories of when they were down and out 60 or even 70 years ago, my dad was the one that helped them, or gave them a chance, or encouraged them.

I just about fell on the floor when someone told me that around 1923 my dad took on the responsibility for an entire family of kids who had an old drunk for a father.

Dad worked all week for 50 cents to buy a big sack of potatoes to feed six kids and himself for the week. I was told that Dad taught the boys of the family trades so they could go out and find work and that these people thought the sun rose and set on my Dad. I had never heard a word about them before my Dad's viewing on July 4th of this year...Oh one more lesson that maybe I didn't learn too well from Dad...don't boast...just do good things.

What's this got to do with great speaking tom?

Well, I'm hoping if you read this far that you saw some value in my Dad's leadership teachings. I'm hoping that when you take the stage that you walk up there as a good example for the many people you will touch in your career. My Dad didn't have the stage in the conventional sense like we do every time we speak. He "lived" the stage. In fact, he "was" the stage that good leadership stands on. Your living example both on the stage and off will be what ultimately makes you a "Great Speaker." I can teach you the techniques, but you must provide the good example 24 hours a day / seven days a week...not just when you are on the platform.

Thanks Dad
Love
Your little "Heapy"

SPEAKERS: Feel free to use any of the examples you see. Even if you just substitute the term "this old man I heard of" for Sam, that's OK. His leadership legacy will live on.

Special thanks to Tom Antion
http://www.GreatInternetMarketingTraining.com

Part 2

Things to Do
After the Funeral

*Life is eternal and love is immortal;
and death is only a horizon, and a
horizon is nothing save the limit of
our sight.*

- Rossiter W. Raymond

Chapter 8

101 Nice Things to Do After the Funeral

You've just attended the funeral of a loved one, friend, relative or acquaintance. Now what? Does it just end there? Is there something you could do that might be a small thing to you, but could be an enormously helpful gesture to the surviving loved ones of the deceased?

This quick list is designed to give you tons of ideas to make the survivors' lives just a little (or a lot) easier after the funeral and in the months of fear, isolation, grieving, and confusion the will most likely follow.

Of course, your knowledge of the person or persons involved will help you select the appropriate items to do and keep you from making the mistake of pushing a little too hard to help out. A gentle nudge to get the person over the hump is probably OK, but you certainly don't want to force someone into something they clearly aren't ready for. Use a heavy dose of discretion.

I've broken down the 101 ideas into several categories and you might see the same idea in several different categories when it's appropriate.

Some the ideas are appropriate immediately after the funeral and some could be used months or even years after the funeral. Hopefully they will be pretty obvious to you. Don't suppose it's a good idea to try to fix someone up with a date for quite a long time after the funeral.

Make sure you read through all categories so you don't miss any ideas that suit you.

Here are the categories:

- ✓ Ideas that will work for just about anyone
- ✓ Ideas if you live close to the survivors

- ✓ Ideas if you live far from the survivors
- ✓ Ideas for very close friends.
- ✓ Ideas for relatives.
- ✓ Ideas for acquaintances / co-workers.
- ✓ Ideas if the survivor is elderly.

*While we are mourning
the loss of our friend,
others are rejoicing
to meet him behind the veil.*

-- John Taylor

Chapter 9

Ideas that will work
for just about anyone

- Give money.

- Send a handwritten note.

- Offer professional advice (only if you're qualified).

- Attend an adult education class with the survivor.

- Keep in touch with the adult children.

- Write a song for the survivor and send a tape or CD.

- Have your entire family sing a song for the survivor and video tape it

- Give a Bible as a gift.

- Bookmark comforting passages in the Bible and send it as a gift.

- Record and send a prayer on tape or CD.

- Sing and record the survivor's favorite religious song ("Amazing Grace," etc.).

- Locate some local support groups for the survivor.

- Find a joke a day on the Internet or out of a joke book and call or email it.

- Show up unexpectedly with a band of people and sing Christmas carols, even if it isn't Christmas.

- Let them hold your baby if it's appropriate (This idea came from a survivor who doesn't even like babies that much. She told me that after her Dad's death she played with one of the relative's babies all day. She said it made her think of life instead of death.)

- Send a live plant.

- Arrange for people to write stories about the deceased. (This idea came from the a survivor who told me that she got an entirely different perspective about her husband after reading stories written about him be his friends. You could coordinate something like this.)

- Get a photo of the deceased or of the deceased's family and make it into a Christmas ornament.

- Donate or participate in deceased's passions, along with survivor. (If the deceased was a big animal advocate. Donate to the local animal shelter in his/her name and/or take the survivor with you and volunteer at the shelter.)

- Write a little booklet about what the deceased meant to you and give it to the survivor.

However long the night,
the dawn will break.

--African Proverb

Chapter 10

Special ideas if you live close to the survivors

- Give pre-cooked food.

- Give pre-cooked food over a couple weeks.

- Go grocery shopping.

- Cut grass.

- Shovel snow.

- Do some fix up projects for the survivor.

- Run errands.

- Provide transportation.

- Lend your car.

- Take over a family business so it doesn't have to be liquidated in distress situation.

- Take the family on a trip.

- Take the kids to the movies.

- Attend an adult education class with the survivor.

- Keep in touch with the adult children.

- Visit and do Bible readings.

- Take the survivor on a shopping spree.

- Have lunch every day with the survivor.

- Take the survivor to play tennis, bridge, bingo etc.

- Decorate/groom the grave site regularly.

- Take the survivor to visit the grave site.

- Locate some local support groups for the survivor.

- Be an ongoing big brother/big sister to the kids.

- Take the kids to school for a week or two.

- Offer to fill in and do things the deceased did, like take grandma to get groceries.

- Fill in for the deceased at mother/daughter, father/son events.

- Show up unexpectedly with a band of people and sing Christmas carols even if it isn't Christmas.

- Take care of the pets for a week or stop by and walk the dog.

- Encourage the survivor to do yoga/meditation and do it with them.

- Take the survivor to an animal shelter and encourage the person to adopt a pet.

Neither fire nor wind,
birth nor death
can erase our good deeds.

-- Buddha (B.C.E. 568-488)

Chapter 11

Special ideas if you live far from the survivors

- Send the survivor handwritten notes each day (This could be for the number of years they were married or some other significant number.)

- Send a handwritten note each week for a year or indefinitely.

- Send funny postcards or greeting cards regularly.

- Email every day or follow the same pattern as your handwritten notes.

- Instant message the survivor with a loving note.

- Arrange for a large group of people to email everyday "We love you. No need to reply"

- Arrange for a large group of people to send notes every week.

- Arrange for a large group of people to call (Make sure you coordinate this and spread out the calls so the survivor isn't overwhelmed one day and has no calls the next.)

- Send funny faxes.

- Send a tiny gift every week.

- Keep in touch with the adult children.

- Send digital and talking photos.

- Write a song for the survivor and send a tape or CD.

- Have your entire family sing a song for the survivor and video tape it.

- Give a Bible as a gift.

- Bookmark comforting passages in the Bible and send it as a gift.

- Record a prayer on tape or CD and send.

- Sing and record the survivor's favorite religious song (Amazing Grace, etc).

- Find a joke-a-day on the Internet or out of a joke book and call or email it.

Birth and Death are the two noblest expressions of bravery.

-- Kahlil Gibran

Chapter 12

Ideas for very close friends

- Offer to take the kids for a week.

- Do the laundry.

- Clean the house.

- Run errands.

- Provide transportation.

- Lend your car.

- Send the survivor handwritten notes each day (This could be for the number of years they were married or some other significant number.)

145

- Send handwritten note each week for a year or indefinitely.

- Send funny postcards or greeting cards regularly.

- Email every day or follow the same pattern as your handwritten notes.

- Instant message the survivor with a loving message.

- Make regular phone calls to the survivor.

- Arrange for a large group of people to email everyday "We love you. No need to reply."

- Arrange for a large group of people to send notes every week.

- Arrange for a large group of people to call (Make sure you coordinate this and spread out the calls so the survivor doesn't get overwhelmed one day and has no calls the next.)

- Send funny faxes.

- Offer to handle all the paperwork like

death certificates, contacting credit card companies, etc.

- Send a tiny gift every week.

- Take over a family business so it doesn't have to be liquidated in a distressful situation.

- Take the family on a trip.

- Take the kids to the movies.

- Spend an evening telling surviving children stories about the deceased from the old days.

- Stay at the house to provide comfort for loneliness.

- Move in permanently.

- Be understanding of the mood swings the survivors may encounter.

- Attend an adult education class with the survivor.

- Keep in touch with the adult children.

- Do a security check on the house.

- Send digital and talking photos.

- Help create a photo album.

- Spend an evening going through old photographs with the survivors.

- Scan many of the old photographs and burn them on a CD or email them.

- Have the old photographs restored electronically and make prints.

- Make a collage of photographs.

- Frame an important photograph.

- Have an important photograph enlarged to poster size.

- Paint a portrait of the deceased / couple either from scratch or from a photograph.

- Sculpt a bust of the deceased.

- Spend an evening with the survivor going through home videos.

- Edit a video of the couple's/deceased's life.

- Supervise the auction of old tools.

148

- Help the survivor sell the deceased's belonging on eBay.

- Write a song for the survivor and send a tape or CD.

- Have your entire family sing a song for the survivor and video tape it.

- Give a Bible as a gift.

- Bookmark comforting passages in the Bible and send it as a gift.

- Record and send a prayer on tape or CD.

- Sing and record the survivor's favorite religious song such as Amazing Grace.

- Visit and do Bible readings aloud.

- Take the survivor on a shopping spree.

- Have lunch every day with the survivor.

- Help set up a remembrance table with pictures of the deceased (My mother has a table like this. It's the same table my Dad sat by for many years as he listened to his books on tape. It has framed pictures of him and my Mom along with other remembrances. They were married 57 years.)

- Set them up on dates. (Make sure the appropriate amount of time has passed on this one. You will have to really be careful not to push too hard. On the other hand, the survivor may secretly want some companionship, but doesn't want to admit it because of guilt. Your extra insistence may allow them to go ahead with it "just to please you or get you off their back.")

- Double date with them.

- Take the survivor to play tennis, bridge, bingo etc.

- Decorate/groom the grave site regularly.

- Take the survivor to visit the grave site.

- Locate some local support groups for the survivor.

- Arrange for a security system and supervise the installation.

- Offer to handle any unexpected details that crop up.

- Offer to handle all the paperwork, on credit card accounts, vehicle titles, etc.

- Offer to handle all the telephone dealings with creditors, bankers, etc.

- Be an ongoing big brother/big sister to the kids.

- Offer to take responsibility for the kids if the surviving spouse passes.

- Offer to fill in and do things the deceased did, like take grandma to get groceries.

- Fill in for the deceased at mother/daughter or father/son events.

- Take the kids to school for a week or two.

- Take care of the pets for a week, or stop by and walk the dog.

- Show up unexpectedly with a band of people and sing Christmas carols even if it isn't Christmas.

- Take the survivor out to exercise, bike ride, tennis, golf, etc.

- Let them hold your baby if it's appropriate (This idea came from a survivor who doesn't even like babies that much. She told me that after her Dad's death she played with one of the relative's babies all day. She said it made her think of life instead of death.)

- Encourage them to volunteer or volunteer with them.

- Encourage journaling.

- Bring funny videos.

- Arrange for people to write stories about the deceased. (This idea came from the a survivor who told me that she got an entirely different perspective about her husband after reading stories written about him be his friends. You could coordinate something like this.)

- Engage the survivor in something "you claim" you need help with. (This will take their mind off their woes for a while.)

- Make a special effort to include the survivor in holiday plans.

- Send a talking picture frame with a loving message.

- Donate or participate in deceased's passions along with survivor. (Let's say the deceased was a big animal advocate. Donate to the local animal shelter in his/her name and/or take the survivor with you and volunteer at the shelter.)

- Send books on coping with grief. (Visit self-help section of book store for many selections.)

- Encourage them to do yoga/meditation and do it with them.

- Take the survivor to an animal shelter and encourage them to adopt a pet that needs them.

- Write a booklet about what the deceased meant to you and give it to the survivor.

We shall find peace.
We shall hear the angels;
we shall see the sky
sparkling with diamonds.

--Anton Chekhov

Chapter 13

Ideas for relatives

- Start trust funds for the young children.

- Offer to take the kids for a week.

- Do the laundry.

- Clean the house.

- Run errands.

- Provide transportation.

- Lend your car.

- Send the survivor handwritten notes each day (This could be for the number of years they were married or some other significant number.)

- Send a handwritten note each week for a year or indefinitely.

- Send funny postcards or greeting cards regularly.

- Email every day or follow the same pattern as your handwritten notes.

- Instant message the survivor with a loving message.

- Arrange for a large group of people to email everyday "We love you. No need to reply"

- Arrange for a large group of people to send notes every week.

- Arrange for a large group of people to call (Make sure you coordinate this so the survivor doesn't get overwhelmed one day and has no calls the next.)

- Send funny faxes.

- Offer to handle all the paperwork like

death certificates, contacting credit card
companies, etc.

- Send a tiny gift every week.

- Take over a family business to prevent it
from being liquidated.

- Take the family on a trip.

- Take the kids to the movies.

- Spend an evening telling surviving
children stories about the deceased from
the old days.

- Stay at the house to provide comfort for
loneliness.

- Move in permanently.

- Move to the area to be closer.

- Be understanding of the mood swings the
survivors may encounter.

- Attend an adult education class with the
survivor.

- Keep in touch with the adult children.

- Perform a security check on the house.

- Send digital and talking photos.

- Help create a photo album.

- Spend an evening looking at old photographs with the survivors.

- Scan many of the old photographs and burn them on a CD or email them.

- Have the old photographs restored electronically and make prints.

- Make a collage of photographs.

- Frame an important photograph.

- Have an important photograph enlarged to poster size.

- Paint a portrait of the deceased / couple either from scratch or from a photograph.

- Sculpt a bust of the deceased.

- Spend an evening with the survivor going through home videos.

- Edit a video of the couple's/deceased's life.

- Supervise the auction of old tools.

- Help the survivor sell the deceased's belonging on eBay.

- Write and record a song for the survivor and send the tape or CD.

- Have your entire family sing a song for the survivor and video tape it.

- Give a Bible as a gift.

- Bookmark comforting passages in the Bible and send it as a gift.

- Record and send a prayer on tape or CD.

- Sing and record the survivor's favorite religious song such as Amazing Grace.

- Visit and read the Bible aloud.

- Take the survivor on a shopping spree.

- Have lunch every day with the survivor.

- Help set up a remembrance table with pictures of the deceased (My mother has a table like this. It's the same table my dad sat by for many years as he listened

to his books on tape. It has framed
pictures of me and my mom along with
other remembrances. They were married
57 years.)

- Set them up on dates (Make sure the
  appropriate amount of time has passed
  on this one. You will have to really be
  careful not to push too hard. On the other
  hand, the survivor may secretly want
  some companionship, but doesn't want to
  admit it because of guilt. Your extra
  insistence may allow them to go ahead
  with it "just to please you or get you off
  their back.")

- Double date with them.

- Take the survivor to play tennis, bridge,
  bingo etc.

- Decorate/groom the grave site regularly.

- Take the survivor to visit the grave site.

- Locate some local support groups for the
  survivor.

- Arrange for a security system and
  supervise the installation.

- Offer to handle any unexpected details that might crop up.

- Offer to handle all the paperwork, on credit card accounts, vehicle titles, etc.

- Offer to handle all the telephone dealings with creditors, bankers, etc.

- Be an ongoing big brother/big sister to the kids.

- Offer to take responsibility for the kids if the surviving spouse passes.

- Offer to fill in and do things the deceased did, like take grandma to get groceries.

- Fill in for the deceased at mother/daughter, father/son events.

- Take the kids to school for a week or two.

- Take care of the pets for a week, or stop by and walk the dog.

- Show up unexpectedly with a band of people and sing Christmas carols even if it isn't Christmas.

- Take the survivor out to exercise, bike ride, tennis or golf.

- Let them hold your baby if appropriate (This idea came from a survivor who doesn't even like babies that much. She told me that after her Dad's death she played with one of the relative's babies all day. She said it made her think of life instead of death.)

- Encourage them to volunteer or volunteer with them.

- Encourage journaling.

- Bring funny videos.

- Arrange for people to write stories about the deceased. (This idea came from the a survivor who told me that she got an entirely different perspective about her husband after reading stories written about him be his friends.

- Engage person in something "you claim" you need help with. (This will take their mind of their woes for a while.)

- Make a special effort to include survivor

in holiday plans.

- Send a talking picture frame with a loving message.

- Donate or participate in deceased's passions along with survivor. (Let's say the deceased was a big animal advocate. Donate to the local animal shelter in his/her name and/or take the survivor with you and volunteer at the shelter.)

- Send book(s) on coping with grief (visit self-help section of book store for many selections.)

- Encourage them to do yoga/meditation and do it with them.

- Take to animal shelter and encourage survivor to adopt a pet that needs them.

- Write a little booklet about what the deceased meant to you.

- Get your entire family involved in staging a tribute play to the deceased.

- Call the survivors regularly.

*Our lives begin to end
the day we become silent
about things that matter.*

--Martin Luther King, Jr.

Chapter 14

Ideas for acquaintances / co-workers

- If you're qualified, offer professional advice.

- Attend an adult education class with the survivor.

- Show up unexpectedly with a band of people and sing Christmas carols even if it isn't Christmas.

- Arrange for friends and co-workers to write stories about the deceased. (This idea came from the a survivor who told me that she got an entirely different perspective about her husband after reading stories written about him be his friends.

- Send a talking picture frame with a loving message.

- Donate or participate in deceased's passions along with survivor. (Let's say the deceased was a big animal advocate. Donate to the local animal shelter in his/her name and/or take the survivor with you and volunteer at the shelter.)

- Write a little booklet about what the deceased meant to you.

- Get your co-workers involved in staging a tribute play to the deceased and video tape it.

- Send an oversize card with the signature of everyone in the company.

Chapter 15

Special ideas if the survivor is elderly

- Stay at the house to provide comfort for loneliness.

- Make regular phone calls.

- Be understanding of the mood swings the survivor may encounter.

- Arrange for emergency paging devices if the survivor will be living alone.

- Help out with electronics like cell phones and DVD players.

- Perform a security check on the house.

- Buy them a computer and help them learn email.

- Send digital and talking photos.

- Help set up a remembrance table with pictures of the deceased (My mother has a table like this. It's the same table my dad sat by for many years as he listened to his books on tape. It has framed pictures of me and my mom, along with other remembrances. They were married 57 years.)

- Arrange for a security system and supervise the installation.

- Let them hold your baby if it's appropriate (This idea came from a survivor who doesn't even like babies that much. She told me that after her Dad's death she played with one of the relative's babies all day. She said it made her think of life instead of death.)

- Encourage them to volunteer or volunteer with them.

- Encourage journaling.

- Bring funny videos.

- Make a special effort to include survivor in holiday plans.

- Send a talking picture frame with a loving message.

- Send a book on coping with grief (Visit the self-help section of a book store for many selections).

- Take to animal shelter and encourage survivor to adopt a pet that needs them.

NOTES

CPSIA information can be obtained at www.ICGtesting.com
Printed in the USA
BVOW04s1847311013

335175BV00008B/210/P